DRAW WITH ♡ GRANDMA

Two-Person Doodle Book

Adam Rusey

CHILD: Draw a tree in different seasons, such as spring and fall.

CHILD

GRANDMA: Draw the tree in summer and winter, to show its transformation.

CHILD: Draw your favorite meal!

CHILD

GRANDMA: Add your grandchild's favorite dessert and some details to the drawing (plates, cups, napkins, glasses).

CHILD: Invent an insect!

CHILD

GRANDMA: Draw the insect making a funny gesture, such as giving a thumb's up or a peace sign.

CHILD: Draw your favorite vehicle!

CHILD

GRANDMA: To make the drawing more dynamic, show the car moving, whether it's racing, turning, or jumping.

GRANDMA

CHILD: Draw one thing you would pack for an adventure! Draw what you're wearing for the adventure!

CHILD

GRANDMA: Sketch one additional item you will require there! Draw any animal companions you might bring along,

GRANDMA

CHILD: Mix birds and animals to create a new hybrid species.

GRANDMA: Add elements to make it funny! (like a unibrow, a mustache, a goofy or shocked look).

GRANDMA

CHILD: Start the drawing with a pair of eyes.

CHILD

RANDMA: Add an element to the drawing. Take turns adding elements back and forth.

GRANDMA

CHILD: Draw a big air balloon!

GRANDMA: Describe the weather! Is it a sunny day or a storm?

GRANDMA

CHILD: Draw a home in outer space!

CHILD

GRANDMA: Who lives there?

CHILD: Draw 2 cupcakes! Add different toppings so that one is very healthy and the other very sweet!

CHILD

GRANDMA: Draw a background (a bakery, a picnic, or a birthday party) to set the scene.

GRANDMA

CHILD: Fill the page with things with wheels!

GRANDMA: Fill the page with things that fly!

GRANDMA

CHILD: Make a drawing just with dots!

CHILD

GRANDMA: Connect the dots and discover the image!

GRANDMA

CHILD: Draw something you're afraid of! Give the object of your fear silly accessories, like a skirt, a hat, or a pair of sunglasses.

CHILD

RANDMA: Draw something you're afraid of! Make it play a game of chess, dance, or do a magic trick.

GRANDMA

CHILD: Draw something that makes you happy!

CHILD

GRANDMA: Draw something that makes you happy!

GRANDMA

CHILD: Draw the biggest birthday cake you can imagine!

CHILD

GRANDMA: Decorate it with your grandchild's favorite candies!

GRANDMA

CHILD: Draw a weird costume!

CHILD

GRANDMA: Who will put on the costume? Include a speech bubble with humorous text!

CHILD: Draw the sky with the biggest rainbow you can imagine!

CHILD

GRANDMA: Draw an unusual treasure at the end of the rainbow!

GRANDMA

CHILD: Draw your favorite season!

CHILD

GRANDMA: Draw your grandchild's favorite activity in that season!

GRANDMA

CHILD: Draw an object you can see right now!

CHILD

GRANDMA: Draw the object you see in an absurd situation. (like a chair floating in mid-air or a lamp growing legs and moving away).

GRANDMA

CHILD: Draw your favorite place in grandma's house.

CHILD

GRANDMA: Add your favorite decorative object.

GRANDMA

CHILD: Draw 3 things that start with the letter "D"!

CHILD

GRANDMA: Draw 3 things that start with the letter "N"!

GRANDMA

CHILD: Draw smiley faces with different expressions! Add different hairstyles for each smiley face!

GRANDMA: Guess what the emotion is for each one! Add elements to make them funny! (like a unibrow, a mustache, sunglasses, a beard).

CHILD: Draw a fruit sliced open!

CHILD

GRANDMA: Imagine a dessert made from the fruit, that your grandchild would like. Draw it!

CHILD: Start the drawing with the outline of a house.

CHILD

GRANDMA: Add an element to the drawing. Take turns adding elements back and forth.

GRANDMA

CHILD: Draw your favorite cartoon character!

CHILD

GRANDMA: Draw a magical creature!

GRANDMA

CHILD: Close your eyes and draw a quick scribble.

GRANDMA: Use the scribble as the starting point for your drawing.

GRANDMA

CHILD: Draw something and then verbally explain to your Grandma exactly how to draw what you have drawn.

CHILD

RANDMA: Is there any resemblance to your grandchild's drawing?

GRANDMA

CHILD: Draw a treasure map.

CHILD

GRANDMA: What does the treasure look like? Draw it!

GRANDMA

CHILD: Draw an animal with superhero abilities!

GRANDMA: Draw villains or enemies who challenge the animal superhero.

CHILD: Draw 5 dots!

CHILD

GRANDMA: Using those dots, draw a person.

CHILD: Draw yourself!

CHILD

GRANDMA: Draw yourself!

GRANDMA

CHILD: Draw your favorite toy!

CHILD

GRANDMA: Draw your favorite toy from your childhood!

GRANDMA

CHILD: Draw a picture of Grandma doing something she loves.

CHILD

GRANDMA: Draw a picture of a favorite family memory.

GRANDMA

CHILD: Draw a Christmas Tree! Add presents underneath the tree.

CHILD

GRANDMA: Add snowflakes or a snowy landscape to create a wintery scene.

GRANDMA

CHILD: Draw a cute cat with a big bow!

CHILD

RANDMA: Show the cat engaging in humorous activities, such as having a tea party, playing an instrument, or surfing.

GRANDMA

CHILD: Start the drawing with a circle.

GRANDMA: Add an element to the drawing. Take turns adding elements back and forth.

GRANDMA

CHILD: Start the drawing with a line!

CHILD

GRANDMA: Add an element to the drawing. Take turns adding elements back and forth.

GRANDMA

CHILD: Draw your favorite winter activity!

CHILD

GRANDMA: Add elements to the background to make it more fun!

GRANDMA

CHILD: If you were an animal, what would it be? Draw it!

CHILD

GRANDMA: Where does it live? Draw the animal's home!

CHILD: Draw your name in fancy letters!

CHILD

GRANDMA: Draw your name with the same
character style!

CHILD: Draw yourself ten years in the future!

CHILD

RANDMA: Draw yourself at your child's age!

GRANDMA

CHILD: Draw the most beautiful flower
bouquet!

CHILD

GRANDMA: Add the most beautiful vase to put the flowers in!

GRANDMA

CHILD: Draw your favorite season!

CHILD

GRANDMA: Draw an activity you would like to do with your grandchild in that season!

GRANDMA

CHILD: Design a maze!

CHILD

GRANDMA: Solve the maze!

GRANDMA

CHILD: Draw an underwater world!

CHILD

GRANDMA: Draw the sky above. How is the weather?

CHILD: Draw an alien!

CHILD

GRANDMA: Draw the alien's granny! What does she wear?

GRANDMA

CHILD: Draw your pet or the pet you would want!

CHILD

RANDMA: Add a pal for this pet! Draw them interacting in a silly or humorous way.

GRANDMA

CHILD: Draw a castle for yourself!

CHILD

GRANDMA: Draw the surrounding landscape.

GRANDMA

CHILD: Fill the page with butterflies!

CHILD

GRANDMA: They are heading to an unexpected place. Draw it!

GRANDMA

CHILD: Draw a silly robot that will help you with some of your tasks.

CHILD

GRANDMA: Draw one task he can accomplish!

GRANDMA

CHILD: Draw a tree!

CHILD

RANDMA: Design a tree house!

Want FREEBIES?

Email Us At:

aideenrusey@gmail.com

Title the email "DRAW WITH GRANDMA" and let us know that you purchased our book.

_____

THANKS FOR YOUR AMAZING SUPPORT!

>>>>>>>>>>>>>>>>>>>>>>>>>>>>>>>>>

For Enquiries and Customer Service
email us at:

aideenrusey@gmail.com

Made in the USA
Columbia, SC
25 November 2024